# INTENTIONOLOGY

*365 Days of Living on Purpose*

**Liz Garrett**

# Enjoy "Intentionology" on Your Phone Completely Free

In gratitude for purchasing this book, and to support your Intention Practice, please enjoy my free gift to you.

Download 12 beautiful images to display prominently on your Lockscreen, Background, or Wallpaper

Go to http://bit.ly/Intentionology to download your images now!

# Do You Have a Book to Write?

**SELF-PUBLISHING**
**SCHOOL**

Discover the EXACT 3-step blueprint you need to
become a bestselling author in 3 months.

Self-Publishing School helped me, and now I want them
to help you with this FREE VIDEO SERIES!

Even if you're busy, bad at writing, or don't know where to start,
you CAN write a bestseller and build your best life.

With tools and experience across a variety of niches and
professions, Self-Publishing School is the only resource
you need to take your book to the finish line.

DON'T WAIT!

Watch this FREE VIDEO SERIES now,
and say "YES" to becoming a best seller:

**Watch the First Video at**
**https://xe172.isrefer.com/go/sps4fta-vts/EWC001**

*To TRUTH,*

*which springs from the heart of every intention.*

# TABLE OF CONTENTS

# ACKNOWLEDGMENTS

I LEARNED ABOUT THE POWER of intention from Dr. Wayne W. Dyer, who said, "Change the way you look at things and the things you look at change."

# INTENTIONOLOGY:
# 365 DAYS OF LIVING ON PURPOSE

B E VERY, VERY CAREFUL. THE seeds of your future are being planted in your psyche right now. Your deepest thoughts will take root and sprout forth as surely as Spring will follow Winter. Look closely: are you planting weeds that will overtake your life, or fruit trees that will delight and nourish?

You get to decide.

Your life experiences have given you a certain set of expectations. Your expectations then color your view, becoming the filter ' through which you experience life. This is natural, but it actually blinds you to experiences that differ from your expectations, guaranteeing you will only see what you expect to see.

This happens to everyone. Here's a trick to overcome it: your mind is always going to be doing something, why not have it work in auto-pilot for your benefit by programming it with positive intentions? An intention is just a sort of mental touchstone, something to return your thoughts to over and over again. Don't worry when your thoughts drift; it is actually the experience and effort of returning to your Intention that strengthens and reinforces it.

## The "-ology" of Intention

What you expect, you experience. This is a deep, deceptively complex truth. It's the way your brain is wired.

The Reticular Activating System (RAS) is the filter through which your brain sorts sensory information. Your brain receives a LOT of information—400 billion bits per second—enough to completely overwhelm your consciousness. You can't consciously react to all that information. So the brain constantly filters the incoming information to make you aware of important information and to store or delete unimportant information. How do you program this filter? With intention! Tell your brain what you want to experience, and it will filter through incoming information and alert you to that experience. Note: the RAS is always working. If you don't consciously program it, it will default to the programming of greatest influence (your childhood, parents, environment, media, etc.).

You've probably had an experience like this: Say, your refrigerator breaks. You open the Saturday paper to look for refrigerator sales and—lo and behold!—there are refrigerator sales everywhere! Ads on several pages. Just for you? No, those ads were always there, but you didn't see them until you set your RAS.

Same is true for the people you experience. If you expect kind people, you'll look for them, and you'll find them. If you expect a-holes, you'll pull them into your awareness.

Same is true for traffic. If you expect ease, you'll experience it. Even if you hit a backup, your creative, powerful brain will draw your attention to ease because that is what you programmed it to do. If you expect frustration, you'll be on the lookout for it, and you'll find it. Either way, your brain will be right.

Intention takes advantage of the Awareness Feedback Loop (depicted below). By getting in the practice of consciously setting your intention, you're using the massive power of your brain to deliver the experience you seek.

Your brain is going to be working anyway, you might as well make it work for you!

Awareness Feedback Loop

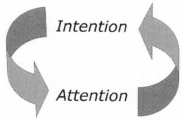

## Living Intentionally

Setting empowering intentions is as simple as deciding what you want to experience in a situation. It can be done at <u>any</u> time for <u>any</u> situation: at the beginning of each day; at any point within any relationship; to manifest a particular project outcome; to affect health conditions; to redirect financial circumstances; to experience pleasant travel; to support specific goals; and, at any point you want to turn around a negative experience. Here are some guidelines for developing empowering intentions:

1. **Empowering Intentions are based in reality**. Intention must relate to the challenge as well as the goal. Intention is not wishing.

2. **Empowering Intentions acknowledge feelings**. Feelings are your friend. They carry a lot of energy, and this energy attracts the object of those feelings. The more you infuse intentions with positive words and meanings that matter to you, the more powerful they will be.

3. **Empowering Intentions focus on moving toward, not away from**. State intentions in terms of what you are manifesting. Avoid the word "not."

4. **Empowering Intentions are stated in the present tense.** State your intention as if it has already come true. Think of it as a reality that already exists which you are now choosing to join.

5. **Empowering Intentions are in alignment with Universal forces.** There are forces greater than you, natural laws that you will not change. Seek to observe and understand these so that your intentions are powered by their flow.

6. **Empowering Intentions require you to claim what is possible for your life.** Sometimes the hardest thing about building a good, happy, productive, fulfilling life is deciding what it will look like . . . and then actively claiming it.

7. **Living Intentionally is POWERFUL.** It activates and directs Universal energy so that you achieve more and experience more pleasure, more joy, and more peace. It creates alignment with reality that results in an ease of life, less struggle. Remember, Intention is a force to reconnect to, not something for ego to accomplish. Intention is about getting into alignment with the Universe, not trying to will things to be.

Let's start now.

Your life opens like an empty canvas before you. What would you like to experience? Begin by developing a vision for the life you desire.

## Process for Writing Empowering Intentions

While you can undertake this as a purely mental process, physically writing your intention amplifies its power many times over. As you begin your day, work through these questions:

1. Looking at your commitments and schedule, are there any opportunities or challenges in this day?

2. Is there anything in your mental, physical or spiritual condition that may limit you today?

3. What would you most like to accomplish today?

4. Given the realities you have identified here, what thought or simple statement could direct and inspire you today? This is your intention!

Here's why living with intention is so powerful: you experience what you expect to experience. Always. This is not to say that intentions "make" things happen. Intentions determine the filter through which you will experience events. By practicing CONSCIOUS intention, you strategically choose expectations that empower you to live a happy and productive life, no matter what happens. You can't control events, but you can control your experience.

Without conscious intention, you will default to the unconscious belief/intention you developed as a defense mechanism when you were a child. What a flat and unempowering way to go through a day! Be careful of your default intention.

Your mind is always working, always talking. By programming it with an empowering intention, you consciously direct it—and your personal resources, and universal forces—toward the life you desire. Your thoughts create your reality, so Intentional Living is about choosing an empowering and positive reality. It becomes a very interesting and rewarding FULL way of life.

## How To Use This Book

**Choose your Intention.** Maybe you're looking for an Intention to serve a particular situation (for example, going into a meeting with a difficult person). Or, maybe you want to direct your awareness for a full day, several days, or a week. You can randomly select an intention, or browse by category to help you meet a specific need. You've found the right Intention when you feel something: hope, peace, excitement, understanding, inspiration. Your heart might beat a little faster. You might smile slightly. You might sigh or even cry. You might feel relief. The Intention that will serve you best carries a slight "charge." When you no longer feel a charge, it's time to find a new Intention.

**Claim your Intention.** Re-write the intention in your own handwriting in the space provided, using words that are meaningful to you and specific to your situation. If it feels good to you, increase the energy of your Intention by using colored inks, designs, images and symbols.

**Proclaim your Intention.** Place your Intention where you will see it often. There are endless creative ways to do this. Carry this book with you. Snap a picture. Memorize and repeat your Intention. Use sticky notes to place Intentions on your computer, refrigerator, visor, and other prominent locations. Write a key word on the palm of your hand. Write your Intention on the note pad you will use during a meeting. Increase the energy of your Intention by sharing it with others, as appropriate, possibly even social media (#Intentionology).

Mark your favorite Intentions by filling in the star. Good Intentions can serve you many times.

**Keep the Process Gentle and Fun.** If you miss a day (or days), no problem! Just resume when you're ready. If an Intention feels slightly "off," no biggie! Just tweak it until it fits. If an Intention makes you struggle, ditch it! Select a different intention. Your brain will lock in the *feeling* of the Intention more than the literal meaning, so give yourself space and permission to enjoy your Intentions.

**Categories**

This book provides 365 Intentions. Some will work for you; some won't. You'll be powerfully attracted to some Intentions immediately, and some won't make sense for years. There will be a few Intentions you go to over and over, and some you will never need. It's all good!

You may seek Intentions to support specific phases or interests, so they're divided into the following categories for easier browsing:

**Alignment** – Everyday intentions that align your awareness with the good of what is, to reduce resistance, and lift you to your higher self.

**Abundance** – Intentions that help keep you in the vibration of Abundance.

**Overcoming Challenges** – Intentions that support the upward journey out of difficult emotional and mental states.

**Specific Day, Date or Occasion** – Intentions anchored in a specific time, event or season.

**Create Your Own** – Prompts and blanks to inspire your intentions.

# INTENTIONS FOR ALIGNMENT

Ahhhhhh, work day is ending. Another transition = another opportunity for intention. I now stop to appreciate and congratulate myself for all I've accomplished today. I allow myself to experience joy and peace this evening.

CK _____

_____

_____

_____

_____ CK

All my planning is secondary. Today I stay tuned to the divine plan for my life.

 C3_____

_____

_____

_____

_____C3

All that must get done, will get done.

I do my part joyfully and easily.

ೞ_____

_____

_____

_____

_____ೞ

Amazing . . . a new day, a new thought,
and everything changes!

૦૩_____

_____

_____

_____

_____ ૦૩

As distractions and demands threaten to pull my focus outward, I strengthen my practice of being centered, Here, Now.

␣ _____

_____

_____

_____

_____ ␣

I see Beauty everywhere.

C/3 _____

_____

_____

_____

_____ C/3

Celebrating others today makes me wonder, shouldn't every day be a birthday?! "Birth" can happen in any moment. Today I celebrate the journey so far and the places yet to go.

ᘓ_____

_____

_____

_____

_____ᘓ

Energies swirl. Forces are at play.

Opportunities open before me.

I greet this week with

CURIOUS EXPECTANCY.

ɔ҃҃_____

_____

_____

_____

_____ ɔ҃

For me, today is a day to contract, restore and renew. Today I let go of all the doings—mine and other's—and simply be.

❧_____

_____

_____

_____

_____❧

God, put me in front of the people

I can serve and show me how.

ଔ_____

_____

_____

_____

_____ ଔ

# Here. Now.

I am clearly well on my way . . .

the stating is the doing.

൫_____

_____

_____

_____

_____൫

I am CONSTANTLY making choices
about my life, my experiences . . .
I consciously choose the direction
I point my choices today.

ᘓ_____

_____

_____

_____

_____ᘓ

I am energetic yet peaceful.

&#8494;_____

_____

_____

_____

_____&#8494;

I am gentle with myself and others.

 og _____

_____

_____

_____

_____ og

I am loving What Is. Everything is as it should be. I have everything I need.

∝_____

_____

_____

_____

_____∝

I am making this a COMPLAINT-FREE day. Today, I release the negative, draining habit that tarnishes my glorious experience.

ᏮᏮ _____

_____

_____

_____

_____ ᏮᏮ

I am not doing this alone.

There are vast resources behind me

and powerful guidance before me.

ℭ₰_____

_____

_____

_____

_____ℭ₰

I am physically strong:

I eat clean, exercise regularly,

get plenty of sleep, and avoid stress.

ෆ_____

_____

_____

_____

_____ෆ

I am practicing being grateful for an outcome BEFORE the outcome.

ങ _____

_____

_____

_____

_____ ങ

I am present. I am listening.

cs _____

_____

_____

_____

_____ cs

I am privileged and grateful for the
opportunity to express my life's mission.

ca_____

_____

_____

_____

_____ca

I am relaxed AND powerful!!!

ા _____

_____

_____

_____

_____ ા

I am shaking up little, unconscious routines (the way I shower, outfit choices, relationship dynamics) to discover deeper, bigger understanding.

ରେ_____
_____
_____
_____
_____ରେ

I am soooooo in love with . . .

THIS . . . MOMENT!

cs _____

_____

_____

_____

_____ cs

I am the detached observer.

ᘓ_____

_____

_____

_____

_____ᘓ

I am the vehicle.

ᶜᵌ_____

_____

_____

_____

_____ᶜᵌ

I am willing to risk good for great.

ɞ_____

_____

_____

_____

_____ɞ

I am wondering . . . what would

happen if . . . even if just for one day . . .

today . . . I allowed myself only to BE . . .

ᘓ‌_____

_____

_____

_____

_____ᘓ

I am willing to accept that I do not see anything or anyone as they really are.

൬_____

_____

_____

_____

_____൬

I ask myself, are my thoughts
and actions IN THIS MOMENT,
moving me toward or away from
trust, love and peace?

ﾂ﾿_____

_____

_____

_____

_____ﾂ﾿

I bravely and faithfully "put it out there"
so the Universe can give me feedback.
This is co-creative give & take.

ଔ_____

_____

_____

_____

_____ ଔ

I breathe deep into my core, detecting and releasing any resistance to my greatness, and greet the day excited and grateful.

ℭʒ_____

_____

_____

_____

_____ℭʒ

I choose my higher behaviors

in every interaction.

CB _____

_____

_____

_____

_____ CB

I claim this day for me: for my renewal, for my replenishment, to hone my focus, to clarify my priorities, to experience love, peace and joy.

 C3

C3

I close my eyes and imagine
my perfect life. I open my eyes
and see the similarities.

ℭ﹍﹍﹍﹍﹍﹍﹍﹍﹍﹍﹍﹍﹍﹍﹍﹍﹍﹍﹍﹍﹍

﹍﹍﹍﹍﹍﹍﹍﹍﹍﹍﹍﹍﹍﹍﹍﹍﹍﹍﹍﹍﹍﹍﹍﹍

﹍﹍﹍﹍﹍﹍﹍﹍﹍﹍﹍﹍﹍﹍﹍﹍﹍﹍﹍﹍﹍﹍﹍﹍

﹍﹍﹍﹍﹍﹍﹍﹍﹍﹍﹍﹍﹍﹍﹍﹍﹍﹍﹍﹍﹍﹍﹍﹍

﹍﹍﹍﹍﹍﹍﹍﹍﹍﹍﹍﹍﹍﹍﹍﹍﹍﹍﹍﹍ℭ

May I be filled with Loving Kindness.

May I be well.

May I be peaceful and at ease.

May I be happy.


(Buddhist prayer)


ℭ₰_____

_____

_____

_____

_____ℭ₰

I decide my mood.

I decide my experience.

I decide my response to others.

ଔ_____

_____

_____

_____

_____ ଔ

I direct my energies to those I can serve and situations I can improve. This is where my gifts are called. If it feels like "a problem," I am not in the right place.

ɞ _____

_____

_____

_____

_____ ɞ

I enjoy the soft comfort

of my familiar body.

ɔ_____

_____

_____

_____

_____ ɔ

I expect good things today.
Whatever happens, I challenge
myself to find the GOOD in it.

&#8484;_____

_____

_____

_____

_____&#8484;

I expect good things.

ଓ_____

_____

_____

_____

_____ ଓ

I expect good.

ଔ _____

_____

_____

_____

_____ ଔ

I feel compelled to "lighten my load:"
my attic, my relationships,
my weight, my beliefs.

CX_____

_____

_____

_____

_____ CX

I feel creative and connected.

ဖ_____

_____

_____

_____

_____ ဖ

I feel excited about the tasks ahead.

ᘓ_____

_____

_____

_____

_____ᘓ

I get what I ask for . . .

do I like what I'm getting?

෦ଃ_____

_____

_____

_____

_____ ෦ଃ

I happily provide

good work to my clients.

ℭ_____

_____

_____

_____

_____ℭ

I hold myself in a place of calm centeredness, seeking to connect to the higher spirit in the person I am talking to, regardless of their words or behavior. I remember, we are all doing the best we can.

ଓ _____

_____

_____

_____

_____ ଓ

I hold the image of my true self clearly in my mind, and the falsehoods fall away.

cx_____

_____

_____

_____

_____cx

I humbly and appreciatively release
my needs to the Universe and receive
its supportive response. I am cared for.
I have everything I need.

Ꮻ_____

_____

_____

_____

_____Ꮻ

I inhale peace, love and abundance.

I exhale worry, fear and scarcity.

cb _____

_____

_____

_____

_____ cb

I intend to have some FUN today!

ᘓ _____

_____

_____

_____

_____ ᘓ

I intend to relax, concentrate, rotate my shoulders, cover the ball, and SHOOT FOR PAR! :)

ଏଓ_____

_____

_____

_____

_____ଏଓ

I joyfully frolic in the flow.

Life is like a water park ride!

_____

_____

_____

_____

_____ଔ

I love my body.

❦_____

_____

_____

_____

_____ ❦

I lovingly enforce limits that honor my body, mind and spirit. There is only so much I can do in a day, and that is okay.

ೞ_____

_____

_____

_____

_____ ೞ

I might as well make the changes
I know I need to make. Life promises,
"Jump . . . or be pushed."

ↂ_____

_____

_____

_____

_____ↂ

I navigate my day, today,

with detached, curious expectancy.

 Cω_____

_____

_____

_____

_____ Cω

I now decide—right now!—to feel good today, all day, no matter what.

ᙏ_____

_____

_____

_____

_____ᙏ

I observe, and release.

ೞ_____

_____

_____

_____

_____ೞ

I offer my experience, abilities and beliefs in loving service to others.

ଔ_____

_____

_____

_____

_____ଔ

I plan my day, and leave empty space
(physical, mental, emotional, spiritual)
for unexpected blessings.

ଓ _____

_____

_____

_____

_____ ଓ

I release all negativity.

_____

_____

_____

_____

_____ C3

I release my puny ideas of what is possible for my life and let the Universe lead me to new ways, new places, new faces, new possibilities. The Universe asks me to step and to trust there will be ground beneath me.

cs_____

_____

_____

_____

_____ cs

I release resistance to what is.

℘ _____
_____
_____
_____
_____℘

I release resistance, judgment and worry
so I can receive Divine Guidance.

Ↄↄ_____

_____

_____

_____

_____Ↄↄ

I release the old to make way for the
new (clean, organize, close-out).

ɔ_____

_____

_____

_____

_____ɔ

I remind myself: the less busy I am,

the more productive I am.

cg

I rest, recover, restore.

I welcome the void. I make space
to imagine possibilities for my self and
my life. I ask my heart what it most
desires. I ask my soul what it longs to
express. I listen to the answer and say,
"Yes!"

&#8476;_____

_____

_____

_____

_____&#8477;

I see you; I hear you;

and what you say matters to me.

ɔჳ_____

_____

_____

_____

_____ɔჳ

I take into this day humble awareness of my own imperfections. I examine the insidious ways I think myself slightly superior to others.

CB _____

_____

_____

_____

_____ CB

I take some time this morning to look at the week ahead—at the meetings and phone calls and encounters—to identify the opportunities to live my mission: (mission statement)

ᚽ_____

_____

_____

_____

_____ᚽ

I trust my wisdom and power.

ଓଃ _____

_____

_____

_____

_____ ଓଃ

I trust the Universe—the right thing always happens. Today I use my organizational ability to make the most of the situation, not to change it.

ෆ_____

_____

_____

_____

_____ ෆ

I used to believe "where there's a will,
there's a way." Now I understand
Will gets in the way. I release
Will to find The Way.

ᴄʒ _____

_____

_____

_____

_____ ᴄʒ

I will not give in to the urge to

RUSH through my day.

ൽ_____

_____

_____

_____

_____ൽ

I wonder what EXCITING things are
going to happen to me today!

CB_____

_____

_____

_____

_____CB

In defenselessness my safety lies.

Today I practice defenselessness.

_____

_____

_____

_____

_____

In every conversation, I wonder,

"How can I inspire and empower?"

I ask, "How can I help you?

ᘓ_____

_____

_____

_____

_____ᘓ

In my busy day, I keep my ears
and eyes tuned to higher guidance.

ଓ _____

_____

_____

_____

_____ ଓ

In this moment, something new . . . in THIS moment, something new . . . and in THIS moment, something new . . . and THIS . . . and THIS . . .

ଔ_____

_____

_____

_____

_____ଔ

It is easy to get lost in the Do Do Do of my day (I do LOVE to check things off a list), but I remind myself to balance it with Be Be Be: Be present, Be real, Be grateful.

ℭ𝔰_____

_____

_____

_____

_____ℭ𝔰

It is my job to hold the vision.

The way will reveal itself.

ന _____

_____

_____

_____

_____ ന

It is up to me to lift the energy of my relationships higher, to honor the holiness that is present between two people. Namaste, my friends.

ༀ_____

_____

_____

_____

_____ༀ

It's Friday—getting across the finish line day—and my intention is to do my best work yet this week, be present and authentic, and create real value for my clients and colleagues.

ભ_____

_____

_____

_____

_____ ભ

Joy courses through me.

 CB _____
_____
_____
_____
_____ CB

Knowing my ripple effect is
infinite, I remind myself to mind
my thoughts and actions.

ℭ_____

_____

_____

_____

_____ℭ

Knowing that the important things always get done, I take some time this morning to make sure I know what's important.

ᘓ_____

_____

_____

_____

_____ᘓ

Let words of empowerment

flow through me today.

ℂ𝔰 _____

_____

_____

_____

_____ ℂ𝔰

Life is fun.

ços

_____

_____

_____

_____

_____ ço

Living with intention is about aligning with Source—not willing things. Today I focus on my connection with greater guidance, opening myself to receive guidance and direction.

ଔ_____

_____

_____

_____

_____ଔ

LOVE is the common
energy that connects all. LOVE is
the energetic basis of all being. LOVE
is the stuff of which we are made.
LOVE pulls us up and toward. This
weekend I give into LOVE.

○ß_____

_____

_____

_____

_____○ß

LOVE MYSELF: I actively listen to the needs of my mind, body and spirit, and honor them.

ೞ _____

_____

_____

_____

_____ ೞ

My attention today goes to the things in my life that are working, giving me pleasure, exciting me, and supporting and sustaining me. Where attention goes, the experience grows!

 beginning _____

_____

_____

_____

_____ beginning

My awareness cuts through the
chaos and distractions to the stillness
within . . . reflecting the stillness of
nature in this season . . . that is
where meaning is.

cx _____

_____

_____

_____

_____ cx

My day is full of pleasures.

I gratefully enjoy them.

ಐ_____

_____

_____

_____

_____ಐ

Today I enjoy and engage in the good humor of the Universe! What if everything is meant to be a joke? Ha!

ଓ _____

_____

_____

_____

_____ ଓ

My home is sanctuary: a place that nourishes and supports me so I can go out into the world with my message.

Ↄ_____

_____

_____

_____

_____Ↄ

My impatience comes from an
erroneous belief that I know how events
are supposed to unfold. Today my
intention is to release impatience, and to
observe, accept and align with the
Universe's plan.

&#8478;_____

_____

_____

_____

_____&#8478;

My innate power is in my connection to the Universe and is activated by CHOICE. When I decide upon an action or a direction, all of the power of the mountains, the sea and the stars gets behind it. Aligning with the Universe is not passive. It requires the input of choice/intention to be part of the flow. When I establish an intention (consciously or not), it becomes the point of great concentrated forces, all converging toward its fruition. Today I constantly, actively choose the higher good.

ങ_____
_____
_____
_____
_____ങ

My intention today is more

a constant prayer: God, help me

accept people as they are.

ભ_____

_____

_____

_____

_____ ભ

My intention today is to

experience clarity and focus.

ᴄ⅃_____

_____

_____

_____

_____ ᴄ⅃

My intention today—Friday!—is to enjoy a sense of completion in my tasks.

○ε _____

_____

_____

_____

_____ ○ε

My life is most joyful and meaningful when I _____.

ଷ_____

_____

_____

_____

_____ଷ

My mission beats my hearts,

breathes my breath, fills my senses.

It is all that I am.

 CB _____

_____

_____

_____

_____ CB

My relationship is jumping to a new level. I release control and responsibility so that we can both blossom.

03_____

_____

_____

_____

_____03

My relationships nurture and inspire me.

ଉ_____

_____

_____

_____

_____ଉ

My theme this week: process &
prioritize. (Let me get clear on my
opportunities and commitments, and
then act on those that are in alignment
with my higher calling.)

ℭℨ_____

_____

_____

_____

_____ℭℨ

My time is mine. I decide
who to give it to and how to use it for
highest good. Today I make responsible
choices about my time.

☙_____

_____

_____

_____

_____☙

My vibration is high. My thoughts know only positive expectations. My eyes turn toward the light.

ℭ_____

_____

_____

_____

_____ℭ

No matter how things may appear,

timing is always perfect.

☙ _____

_____

_____

_____

_____ ☙

p.e.a.c.e.

5 letters = 5 fingers.

I tap it out all day long like a

meditative metronome.

p.e.a.c.e.

ᚳ _____

_____

_____

_____

_____ ᚳ

Peace to me. Peace to family.

Peace to friends. Peace to the world.

൭_____

_____

_____

_____

_____൭

Peace and joy are on my mind this week. Such powerful energies! Whenever I am able to experience peace and joy in my heart, I am helping to heal myself, others and the planet. I notice and release discord within. Even a millisecond of peace, because it is so powerful, can change everything.

CЗ_____

_____

_____

_____

_____CЗ

Putting in place my centering
practices for the busy week ahead:
journaling, yoga, meditation, essential
oils, outside activity and, of course,
conscious intention.

ᴄꜱ_____

_____

_____

_____

_____ᴄꜱ

Respecting the cycles of energy, today I rest, relax, renew and ENJOY a beautiful day . . . no matter what others might imagine for me.

 CB _____

_____

_____

_____

_____ CB

TENDERNESS is my theme today . . . for myself and those I encounter (or think of). Everyone could use a little tenderness.

ଔ_____

_____

_____

_____

_____ ଔ

The less I speak, the more I see.

809_____

_____

_____

_____

_____809

The Universe affirms my efforts and, as a result, I experience busyness. Today I keep very focused on completing the tasks that are most in alignment with my mission.

ℭ𝔰_____

_____

_____

_____

_____ℭ𝔰

The urge to run head-first into and through all these To Do's is strong. I stop. I consciously choose my next action based on MY priorities.

ᘓ_____

_____

_____

_____

_____ᘓ

There is magic everywhere! . . .
including within me. Today I'm playing
with magic (and it's playing back).

CƐ_____
_____
_____
_____
_____CƐ

There is nothing that replaces
good sleep. I am reminded, my
first responsibility is to myself. I can't
give to the world if I don't take care
of myself first. Today I make
sure my needs are met.

☙_____

_____

_____

_____

_____☙

Things get done easily,

almost effortlessly.

This day is a gift, especially
for me! Even before I look
into the box, what I see is what
I get. I decide now what I will
see in the gift of today.

℃ﾞ_____

_____

_____

_____

_____℃ﾞ

Today I am a passenger, letting the
Universe take me where I need to go
and show me what I need to see.

○ʒ_____

_____

_____

_____

_____○ʒ

Today I am paying attention to how my choices feel . . . living with intention in alignment with purpose feels GOOD. Feeling good tells me I'm on the right path. Feeling fearful, upset, sad or angry tells me I need to make a different choice.

ℭ_____

_____

_____

_____

_____ℭ

Today I am realistic about the grid of time, managing my 24 blocks of it with meaningful, intentional activity, loving and appreciating every minute I get, and letting the unimportant stuff fall away.

ᙟ_____

_____

_____

_____

_____ᙟ

Today I celebrate the FOOL within me,
the trusting, silly, childlike aspect that
knows the importance of fun and
laughter and risking self. Viva la fool!

 са _____

_____

_____

_____

_____ са

Today I continue to enjoy the power of being present in the Now, of focusing my thoughts and energy on the highest good in this instance, and feeling flooded with gratitude for the fullness of this ever-unfolding, continuous moment.

ɔ﹍﹍﹍﹍﹍﹍﹍﹍﹍﹍﹍﹍﹍﹍﹍﹍﹍﹍﹍

﹍﹍﹍﹍﹍﹍﹍﹍﹍﹍﹍﹍﹍﹍﹍﹍﹍﹍﹍﹍

﹍﹍﹍﹍﹍﹍﹍﹍﹍﹍﹍﹍﹍﹍﹍﹍﹍﹍﹍﹍

﹍﹍﹍﹍﹍﹍﹍﹍﹍﹍﹍﹍﹍﹍﹍﹍﹍﹍﹍﹍

﹍﹍﹍﹍﹍﹍﹍﹍﹍﹍﹍﹍﹍﹍﹍﹍﹍﹍ɔ

Today I drop the fears and worries and judgments that separate me from others. It always comes down to this: just love.

03_____

_____

_____

_____

_____03

Today I enjoy the satisfaction of

completing good work . . . early! . . .

and then I enjoy "free" time.

I am motivated!

ᘓ_____

_____

_____

_____

_____ᘓ

Today I enjoy the strength
and perfection of my body.

ᘓ_____

_____

_____

_____

_____ᘓ

Today I experience and express beauty.

 CB _____

_____

_____

_____

_____ CB

Today I experience fulfillment
in my work by smiling and enjoying
the tasks I choose to do.

ᘉ_____

_____

_____

_____

_____ᘉ

Today I focus on the newness in my day. There is so much! It is refreshing to see new possibilities.

cs _____

_____

_____

_____

_____ cs

Today I focus on thoughts and actions that move me forward.

ℭ₰_____

_____

_____

_____

_____ℭ₰

Today I give a gift to

everyone I encounter.

CB_____

_____

_____

_____

_____CB

Today I give careful attention to my pace of living, allowing relaxation and peace while, at the same time, getting things done with right-timing.

ଓ_____

_____

_____

_____

_____ଓ

Today I give my precious energy
ONLY to my priorities (and not
those little thieves that disguise
themselves as "urgencies").

ञ‍_____

_____

_____

_____

_____ ञ‍

Today I hit the "pause" button, halting my scattered forward motion long enough to process and organize all the To Do's that vie for my attention, committing only to those that truly represent my priorities and values.

Ↄ&_____

_____

_____

_____

_____ Ↄ&

Today I keep my eyes and ears and HEART open to new opportunities.

ଓ_____

_____

_____

_____

_____ଓ

Today I keep my head in my chosen work. My walls are impenetrable to the energy drains of interruptions, unproductive thoughts, and other people's ideas of what I should be doing with my time. I am the boss of me.

cs _____

_____

_____

_____

_____ cs

Today I let go of thoughts and
beliefs and reactions and defenses
that no longer serve me.

ભ_____

_____

_____

_____

_____ભ

Today I look to add value to every situation and give my gift to every person, intentionally leaving places, people and things a little better than I found them.

☙_____

_____

_____

_____

_____☙

Today I look to add value to every situation and give my gift to every person, intentionally leaving places, people and things a little better than I found them.

ɔ_____

_____

_____

_____

_____ ɔ

Today I manage my precious personal energy by pointing my awareness to that which energizes me and away from that which drains me.

 CЗ_____

_____

_____

_____

_____CЗ

Today I notice how much laughter

surrounds me—more than I knew!

cx_____

_____

_____

_____

_____cx

Today I notice my choices
(big and small) and the points of
empowerment they offer.

ॐ_____

_____

_____

_____

_____ॐ

Today I notice the meaning

I assign to things.

ଔ_____

_____

_____

_____

_____ଔ

Today I notice WITH DEEP
GRATITUDE the constant stream
of good things that come to me.

ᙅ_____

_____

_____

_____

_____ᙅ

Today I observe what it means

to get back what I put out.

ଓ_____

_____

_____

_____

_____ଓ

Today I practice coming present and asking, "God, how would you have me serve this person?"

 CB_____

_____

_____

_____

_____CB

Today I practice forgiveness.
As I perceive shortcomings in myself
and others, I release judgment, and
choose instead to love.

ᢒᔓ_____

_____

_____

_____

_____ᢒᔓ

Today I practice honoring the
truth in THIS moment. Let me be
filled with loving kindness.

Ↄ_____

_____

_____

_____

_____Ↄ

Today I radiate warmth . . . a
caring smile, real eye contact, heartfelt
laughter. I experience warmth all
around me. I enjoy warmth.

cs _____

_____

_____

_____

_____ cs

Today I really will complete those "high priority" items on my To Do list . . . really!

൪_____

_____

_____

_____

_____൪

Today I re-dedicate myself to
my mission (again and again . . .).
I make it the MOST important thing.

ଓ_____

_____

_____

_____

_____ ଓ

Today I refrain from
"should-ing" myself and others.
Who am I to know "should"?

ભ_____

_____

_____

_____

_____ ભ

Today I remember I am in a
co-creative relationship. I do my
part, and receive with gratitude and
amazement Spirit's part.

ↄ｝_____

_____

_____

_____

_____ↄ｝

Today I remember that I can
fly . . . and that it is up to me to
flap my arms and leap.

ᘓ_____

_____

_____

_____

_____ᘓ

☆

Today I remind myself,

living my mission is a matter of

(spiritual) life and death!

ᴓ______________________________

______________________________

______________________________

______________________________

______________________________ᴓ

Today I respect my body's request

(demand?) to rest, recover and restore.

Ↄ_____

_____

_____

_____

_____Ↄ

Today I run eagerly toward
the opportunities to do good,
satisfying, rewarding work.

൫_____

_____

_____

_____

_____൫

Today I scrupulously eye my schedule and tasks to make sure they express MY priorities.

ೞ_____

_____

_____

_____

_____ ೞ

Today I slow my reaction time down.

As I count to 3 (or more), I notice

messages from my body or intuition.

In all interactions, I am loving and kind.

cx _____

_____

_____

_____

_____ cx

Today I stay clear and
committed to my priorities.

CB _____

_____

_____

_____

_____ CB

Today I stay present with
What Is. Without judgement.
Without attachment.

ⱽꙄ_____

_____

_____

_____

_____ⱽꙄ

Today I take time to

reconnect with the Divine.

ﾍ_____

_____

_____

_____

_____ﾍ

Today I treat myself kindly . . .

thoughts, words, choices, actions . . .

so I can truly be kind to others.

ങ‌_____

_____

_____

_____

_____ങ‌

Today I trust that what
"must" get done will get done.
(By definition, it always does.)

_____

_____

_____

_____

_____ ଓ3

Today I will not say, "I'm tired."

CZ _____

_____

_____

_____

_____ CZ

Today is not about getting things done, checking things off, or just getting through it all. It is about feeling the fire within, no matter what.

ભ_____

_____

_____

_____

_____ભ

Today is perfect, as always.

It is my job to remember that.

ↈ_____

_____

_____

_____

_____ↈ

Today is YES . . . and THANK YOU.

ભ_____

_____

_____

_____

_____ ભ

Today my attention is on

the upward trend of things.

 CG_____

_____

_____

_____

_____CG

Today my focus is on
accurately and authentically expressing
myself, especially through spoken
and written word.

 george_____

_____

_____

_____

_____george

Today will be filled with opportunities to be helpful to people. Let it be an active meditation for me.

 C3 _____

_____

_____

_____

_____C3

Today, I am present to the adventure,

the newness in this Now.

ℭ _____

_____

_____

_____

_____ℭ

Today, I appreciate common beauty.

ᙢ _____

_____

_____

_____

_____ ᙢ

Today, I keep my attention inward.

ୡ_____

_____

_____

_____

_____ୡ

Today, I look for the good.

ᏻ_____

_____

_____

_____

_____ᏻ

Today, I share beauty.

 CB_____

_____

_____

_____

_____ CB

Today, I spend 95% of my
time on my top 5 priorities.

ℭ _____

_____

_____

_____

_____ ℭ

Today, I stay present and
focused on my inner experience,
and leave others to theirs.

 CЗ_____

_____

_____

_____

_____CЗ

Today, in my mind, I secretly
and constantly say I LOVE YOU
to every person I meet, see, hear about,
think of, or share the planet with
(and the animals, and trees, and
skys, etc., etc., etc.)

ଔ_____

_____

_____

_____

_____ଔ

Trusting my body's wisdom,
today I am motivated by what makes
me feel good. I have made the decision
that I will feel GOOD today!

ↃↃ_____

_____

_____

_____

_____ↃↃ

What choice can I make in this
moment (and this . . . and this . . .) that
will allow me to experience JOY now?

ℭ_____

_____

_____

_____

_____ℭ

What comes to me comes for my good . . . whether or not I understand it, whether or not I like it, whether or not really believe that. Today, I endeavor to gratefully receive whatever comes.

ℂℰ_____

_____

_____

_____

_____ℂℰ

What if the Universe is speaking to me in poetry, and everything I experience is a metaphor?!

ᙢ_____

_____

_____

_____

_____ᙢ

What keeps me from trusting my intuition? Judgment of the information it offers. Today I practice dropping all judgment.

 CB _____

_____

_____

_____

_____ CB

What thoughts am I believing
in this moment? What is the
experience that results?

cx_____

_____

_____

_____

_____cx

When I look at the long list of little To Do's in front of me today, I see I have many opportunities to positively affect people's lives. Seeing things this way brightens what could otherwise be a very dull day.

 C03 _____

_____

_____

_____

_____ CO3

With grace and gratitude, I let go and clear out old energies, possessions, commitments, practices, routines and beliefs that no longer serve me.

○�_____

_____

_____

_____

_____○჻

Yes, I will meet the demands of my various roles today, all the while keeping my awareness of my core connection with something greater.

ೞ_____

_____

_____

_____

_____ೞ

Today I give myself permission
to work on the things I enjoy.

ભ_____

_____

_____

_____

_____ભ

I revel in the newness of today, the fresh opportunities in each never-seen-before moment. I release expectation, pre-judgment and knowingness so that I am empty and open to the full experience of Now.

ख_____

_____

_____

_____

_____ख

Today I remember my co-creative role in my life. I make the best choices I know how to incrementally move myself into alignment with Spirit.

ༀ_____

_____

_____

_____

_____ༀ

Today I ride my creativity like a surfer rides the waves: one with its ups and downs; absorbed in its energy; cutting my path within the bounds of where it will take me; aware; joyful!

 Cℛ_____

_____

_____

_____

_____ Cℛ

Today I challenge myself to
be connected and creative in this
NOW (regardless of who/what/
where surrounds me).

CB_____

_____

_____

_____

_____CB

# INTENTIONS FOR ABUNDANCE

Abundance comes with
the support and resources needed to
accommodate abundance! I gratefully
receive abundance.

CB_____

_____

_____

_____

_____CB

Abundance is not given. It is
not a reward or a result of my efforts.
It cannot be withheld. Abundance just
IS. My job is to receive it. Today I enjoy
the natural state of abundance.

 G_____

_____

_____

_____

_____G

Counting my blessings today . . . I'm gonna need to borrow fingers and toes.

ଔ_____

_____

_____

_____

_____ଔ

For the benefit of myself and others,

I receive abundance now.

ᘓ_____

_____

_____

_____

_____ᘓ

Holding the vision . . .
feeling the vision . . . charging
the vision . . . living the vision.

ଔ_____
_____
_____
_____
_____ଔ

I am actively listening for the answer to the question I asked the Universe: What should I be doing NOW to fulfill my life's mission?

cs_____

_____

_____

_____

_____cs

I am an opportunity magnet! I make myself ready to receive the exciting new possibilities flying my way.

൙_____

_____

_____

_____

_____൙

I am open to guidance to develop
new thinking that welcomes the
abundance that floods my life now.

ۛ_____

_____

_____

_____

_____ۛ

I am powerful. My power is NOW.

I am present to my powerful self.

ℭ𝔰_____

_____

_____

_____

_____ℭ𝔰

I let go of limiting beliefs
and thoughts so that my hands are free
to receive the gifts and opportunities
coming my way. All day, I ask myself,
"What can I let go NOW?"

ca _____

_____

_____

_____

_____ ca

I do not hurry,

yet everything is accomplished.

 CB _____

_____

_____

_____

_____ CB

I hold detailed, emotionally-
charged images of success in my mind.
What I expect, I will experience.

Ↄ_____
_____
_____
_____
_____Ↄ

I hold the vision . . . and do the work.

ჯ_____

_____

_____

_____

_____ ჯ

I know I will be receiving

gifts all day! Can't wait!

ↀ_____

_____

_____

_____

_____ↀ

I live in wealth and abundance.

Money is a positive experience.

ଔ_____

_____

_____

_____

_____ ଔ

I now step into the BIG LIFE

the Universe intends for me!

ఴ_____

_____

_____

_____

_____ ఴ

I plant seeds everywhere, joyfully cultivating new creative, well-paying opportunities. I view the future with curious expectancy—what fabulous opportunities are coming next?

ॐ_____
_____
_____
_____
_____ॐ

I relax in the confidence
of knowing everything I need to
succeed is already provided.

ᗡ_____
_____
_____
_____
_____ᗡ

I release the falsehood that
depletion is necessary to justify inflow.
Abundance is not conditional.

 beginning of line _____

_____

_____

_____

_____ end

I watch in amazement as

my intentions are granted . . .

and multiplied! I am grateful.

New opportunities arrive to
fill the void my mind/body/spirit
clearing created—I am excited and
grateful. With curious expectancy I
wonder, where am I being led now?

 CB_____

_____

_____

_____

_____CB

OPEN is my state of being today.

Open to: experience, opportunity,

friendships, conversations, possibilities!

ℂℨ_____

_____

_____

_____

_____ℂℨ

So many people ahead
of me on the path today—I can't
wait to discover them.

 CB
_____
_____
_____
_____
_____CB

The cycle of abundance
begins and ends with gratitude.

ோ_____

_____

_____

_____

_____ஸ

The Universe seeks to grant my wants, so I am careful and clear about my wants (especially those limiting, fearful wants that hide in dark corners). Today I claim my wants clearly and specifically.

ભ_____

_____

_____

_____

_____ભ

To overcome my "negativity bias," I keep my thoughts focused on the experiences I want and the abundance surrounding me.

ↈ_____
_____
_____
_____
_____ↈ

Today I identify and
organize (and maybe prioritize)
the many opportunities that are
swirling around me.

ℭ‍ß_____

_____

_____

_____

_____ℭ‍ß

Today I keep my head and
heart filled with good (and notice
how I attract even more good).

ෆ_____
_____
_____
_____
_____ෆ

Today I list 100 ways my
dreams are manifesting NOW.

ᙢ_____

_____

_____

_____

_____ ᙢ

I stay focused on my mission,

knowing all will be provided.

અ_____

_____

_____

_____

_____અ

Show up. Shut up. Serve.

CB _____

_____

_____

_____

_____ CB

My way is clear to me and not
influenced by (imagined or real)
temptations or threats by others.

I am grateful for the comforts

I continually experience.

ദ_____

_____

_____

_____

_____ദ

I am worthy, right here, right now.

ᘓ_____

_____

_____

_____

_____ᘓ

I deliver value just by
being authentically me.

Just like the lilies in the field,

my needs are met.

ଔ_____
_____
_____
_____
_____ଔ

Abundance flows to me and
through me. I receive. I give.

ॐ_____

_____

_____

_____

_____ॐ

I notice how easily my problems resolve and my needs disappear.

ა_____

_____

_____

_____

_____ა

I allow abundance, here, now.

 og _____

_____

_____

_____

_____ og

I bless the money I spend

so that it serves the world.

ജ_____

_____

_____

_____

_____ജ

Today I receive. Whatever information, support, and resources that come my way—whether or not I understand or think I need—I say YES to. This is the Universe lifting me higher.

ᘓ _____

_____

_____

_____

_____ ᘓ

Today I visualize my success,
imagining with full sensory detail that
my goals have been attained. I already
am all I desire to be!

०३ _____

_____

_____

_____

_____ ०३

Whatever I imagine, the Universe provides. Today I IMAGINE thoroughly, positively, deeply, expansively, wildly and joyfully!

 Cß_____

_____

_____

_____

_____Cß

# INTENTIONS FOR
# OVERCOMING CHALLENGES

I am never alone. When events challenge me, I see how much I can let go of (possessions, commitments, relationships, beliefs, expectations, etc). I seek stillness so I can hear what the Universe is trying to tell me. And then I heed it—no matter how difficult—because life has taught me to trust the voice that comes from the still, quiet place inside.

ᘓ_____

_____

_____

_____

_____ᘓ

(Your Name), whatever you say
and do today will be enough.

൫_____

_____

_____

_____

_____൫

(Though tempted by not feeling well today, lack of sleep, chaos in my schedule and worries about a loved one) Today I keep turning my mind back to the good in this moment.

 CB _____

_____

_____

_____

_____ CB

Amidst the chaos, I keep my ears and
eyes tuned to higher guidance.

 CB _____

_____

_____

_____

_____ CB

As I let go of that which holds
me down, I become buoyant.
I release . . . I float.

ᛤ_____

_____

_____

_____

_____ᛤ

Difficult conversation
approaching. I set my intention:
speak from love or not at all.

CB _____

_____

_____

_____

_____ CB

Doing more of the same (even if harder and harder) and expecting different results is CRAZY. Today I change things up. Bah-bye old and hello new.

ℭ_____

_____

_____

_____

_____ℭ

Doubt appears like weeds in
my garden. Do I pluck them out without
regard to the depth of their roots, or do
I let them show me their special flower?
Today I sit with doubt.

&#8531;_____

_____

_____

_____

_____&#8531;

Email, you don't own me. This week I process email on MY schedule, in decided time-blocks, as my energy and interest allow.

ⳞⳠ_____

_____

_____

_____

_____ⳞⳠ

Even though I am angry

and disappointed about a situation I

must confront today, I remind myself

to engage with kindness and humility.

We are all just humans doing

the best we can.

 CB_____

_____

_____

_____

_____ CB

Facing a challenge today,
I remember, the good is not always
apparent, but it is there. Wait and
watch, and it will be revealed.

ଔ_____

_____

_____

_____

_____ଔ

Faulty thinking is always the cause of my discontent. Today I practice tracing undesired experiences to their roots and removing them there.

ﾌﾞ_____

_____

_____

_____

_____ﾌﾞ

Forgiveness isn't something I do. It is a grace I allow to move through me.

ભ_____

_____

_____

_____

_____ ભ

How is your day going? The beauty of using intention is that you can change your experience by changing your thoughts at any time. Even now.

✂ _____
_____
_____
_____
_____ ✂

I am in awe of our innate drive toward healing . . . physically, mentally, emotionally, spiritually . . . the direction is always toward wholeness.

ᘓ_____

_____

_____

_____

_____ᘓ

I could be resentful for having to work on a Sunday, but instead I choose to be GRATEFUL. This is what living with intention is—finding the higher truth and pointing yourself to it.

C3 _____

_____

_____

_____

_____ C3

I focus my attention, laser-like,

on the insidious ways I complain (the

weather, not feeling well, criticisms and

judgments, not enough time/energy/

money/whatever, discomforts,

discontents, dislikes, etc) and cut those

cancers out, leaving a healthy

and robust appreciation for the

perfection of what is.

ᛦ_____

_____

_____

_____

_____ᛦ

I gratefully rise to the opportunities presenting themselves. Everything I need to succeed is provided.

ℭ∫_____

_____

_____

_____

_____ ℭ∫

I have been distracted lately.

Now, I slowly and gently, little by little,

using my tools, return my focus to

my higher connection.

ཅ§_____

_____

_____

_____

_____§ཅ

I keep bringing myself back to 100%—there is no partial belief, no partial faith—either I'm all-in, or I'm out. I'm choosing all-in.

ca _____

_____

_____

_____

_____ ca

I let go so the right thing can happen.

cs _____

_____

_____

_____

_____ cs

I need guidance. I put my
questions to the Universe and watch,
curious and open, for answers.

ख_____

_____

_____

_____

_____ख

I now stop the exhausting push forward,

and allow myself to be pulled.

ఆ_____

_____

_____

_____

_____ ఆ

I pull my thoughts from the whirling, sucking vortex of tasks and obligations and worries, and point them high, over and over again.

ɞ_____

_____

_____

_____

_____ɞ

I release others to their
paths as I focus on my own.

_____

_____

_____

_____

_____

I release the struggle. In this
moment, all is as it should be.

I respect my cycles of expansion and contraction, honoring what is without trying to change it.

ભ_____

_____

_____

_____

_____ભ

I stay within the bounds
of what I can control: me. I release
others to their path.

CB_____
_____
_____
_____
_____CB

In my co-creative relationship with ☆ the Universe, I am responding to feedback that I must do things differently. DIFFERENT is not failure. DIFFERENT is necessarily uncomfortable. DIFFERENT is part of change (without DIFFERENT everything remains the same). Today I embrace DIFFERENT.

 CB _____

_____

_____

_____

_____ CB

In this moment, what is

asking for acceptance?

CX _____

_____

_____

_____

_____ CX

Many tasks and people vie for my attention today. Although I am tempted by the distraction and ego-gratification they offer, I remain committed to my priorities. First things first.

ଔ_____

_____

_____

_____

_____ଔ

My mind is fertile soil. I decide
which seeds take root and flourish.

cs _____

_____

_____

_____

_____ cs

My path leads me to greater
and greater authenticity. I appreciate the
opportunities today brings to be true to
who I am NOW, and to act in loving
kindness toward family and friends who
bless my life. I am grateful, Here, Now.

ɔ₃_____

_____

_____

_____

_____ɔ₃

My spirituality has grown

forth from my struggles.

൘ _____

_____

_____

_____

_____ ൙

Negative thought never ever ever ever ever ever ever ever serves me. Today, I pluck them like weeds.

&#x2053;_____

_____

_____

_____

_____&#x2053;

☆

No matter what chaos surrounds me, there is always a peaceful calm center within. Over and over, I return there.

No matter what comes, my intention is to experience trust, love and peace.

ɔ̃_____

_____

_____

_____

_____ ɔ̃

On days when I can't quite keep my thoughts on my highest ideals, it is still quite empowering and experience-altering to at least keep them out of the ditch. I'm doing my best.

ଔ_____

_____

_____

_____

_____ ଔ

Putting one foot in front of the other . . . one action leading to the next and the next and the next . . . as I am able, willing and ready . . . heading slowly but steadily toward my heart's desires.

Remember, remember, remember:
we are not alone. Guidance is always
available. Our needs are provided for.
In each moment, all is good. Try
to remember this today.

ℭ_____
_____
_____
_____
_____ℭ

The "demands" upon me are really opportunities. Let me greet them with curious expectancy. What is being offered to me (vs taken from me)?

 C3_____

_____

_____

_____

_____C3

Things are always changing, and that involves the LOSS of what has been known and the GAIN of the unfamiliar. Change is inevitable, unstoppable, impartial and unavoidable. Resistance is a waste of precious energy. Today I see change for the ally it is, making me grow, keeping me fresh. When I see loss and gain, I say, "oh, there's my friend, Change."

ᘓ_____

_____

_____

_____

_____ᘓ

Though the river is sometimes rough,

I know I am cradled and guided.

ᑲ_____

_____

_____

_____

_____ᑲ

To really make change in my life, it makes no sense to keep doing the same things harder. Today, I continually ask, "What can I do differently to create the change I desire?"

CB _____

_____

_____

_____

_____ CB

Today I allow forgiveness

to enter Here and Now.

ଙ୍ଗ_____

_____

_____

_____

_____ ଙ୍ଗ

Today I get to practice being okay
(staying centered, peaceful and loving)
while experiencing the disapproval of an
important person. If I am true,
outcome will be true.

ℭ _____
_____
_____
_____
_____ ℭ

Today I keep my focus on the
things that bring me up, and trust the
problems will (a) work themselves out,
(b) go away, or (c) present a clear
opportunity for action.

&#8494;_____

_____

_____

_____

_____&#8494;

Today I listen more to that
wise guidance that comes from deep
within and beyond me, and less to the
fearful clamor of my mind.

CB _____

_____

_____

_____

_____CB

Today I must be present with truths that cause pain. How? Drop judgment. Believe in good. Be curious, open. Be grateful. All is good, always.

ぐ⊱_____
_____
_____
_____
_____⊱

Today I practice TOLERANCE by reminding myself, "It's not about me."

ᛦ_____

_____

_____

_____

_____ᛦ

Today I remember: obstacles are what I see when I take my eye off my goal.

ᏣᏣ_____

_____

_____

_____

_____ ᏣᏣ

Today I respect the capacity

of my "5 pound bag."

ભ_____

_____

_____

_____

_____ભ

Today, let me get clearer on the truths I'd rather avoid. I need to see—and embrace—them too.

cx _____

_____

_____

_____

_____ cx

Today, the best that I can do given the circumstances, is to keep moving. This is the only way the Universe can give me feedback on my efforts.

 CB_____

_____

_____

_____

_____CB

Upset surrounds me. I must work
hard to protect my joy today.

ᗧ_____

_____

_____

_____

_____ᗧ

We often confuse the Universe's loving "feedback" with the cruel falsehood known as "failure." Today, say THANK YOU UNIVERSE, no matter what.

൙_____

_____

_____

_____

_____ ൙

What will it be, CHANGE or
MORE OF THE SAME? This is
decided in each moment.

ᎤᏰ_____

_____

_____

_____

_____ᎤᏰ

When I am able to be very present in the moment, I find everything I need.

When my day does not seem
to be going "right," I remember the
Universe is giving me exactly what
I need. I humble myself in
order to receive it.

ↄ﹌﹌﹌﹌﹌﹌﹌﹌﹌﹌﹌﹌﹌﹌﹌﹌﹌

﹌﹌﹌﹌﹌﹌﹌﹌﹌﹌﹌﹌﹌﹌﹌﹌﹌

﹌﹌﹌﹌﹌﹌﹌﹌﹌﹌﹌﹌﹌﹌﹌﹌﹌

﹌﹌﹌﹌﹌﹌﹌﹌﹌﹌﹌﹌﹌﹌﹌﹌﹌

﹌﹌﹌﹌﹌﹌﹌﹌﹌﹌﹌﹌﹌﹌ↄ

Why do I carry these hurts and defenses around like buckets of rocks, reducing my power, limiting my ability, exhausting me? I set these buckets down NOW knowing, should I ever desire to pick them back up, they will be there. This is the choice I practice today.

ᑯ_____

_____

_____

_____

_____ᑯ

Yes, there are rhythms in life
and they don't always feel good,
but we can embrace them for the
release and opportunity they offer.
Blessings to you as you exhale.

ↈ_____

_____

_____

_____

_____ↈ

Yes, well, life happens. Living with intention is making the most of our reality, not ignoring it. C'est la vie!

CB_____

_____

_____

_____

_____CB

# Intentions for a Specific Day, Date or Occasion

A new month—a new beginning—what would you like this month to hold for you?

℘ _____

_____

_____

_____

_____℘

As I face change and uncertainty in my day, I am comforted to remember the trees have lost their leaves, preparing, in the most natural of cycles, for renewal, as am I.

ભ_____

_____

_____

_____

_____ભ

Christmas begs for benchmarking. Memories of Christmases past tell us where we've been, and our hopes tell us where we want to go. Good information for action in the Now. What will this Christmas be for me?

ᘓ_____

_____

_____

_____

_____ᘓ

Filled with expectant

curiosity for the new year!

�☙_____

_____

_____

_____

_____ ❧

Gratitude is one of the most powerful energies you can conjure. November is perfect for strengthening your gratitude practice—doing specific things daily that increase your enjoyment of life. Keep a gratitude list today.

○ß_____

_____

_____

_____

_____○ß

Here comes one of the most influential, fertile transition times: the new year. Prepare to make the most of this opportunity. Look deep inside now. What cries for expression in the coming year? Give it voice: say it out loud, tell friends, write it down, post it here. Be brave—the Universe will push you toward your success if you just take the first steps.

 C3 _____

_____

_____

_____

_____ C3

Here we are at week's end.
How do you want this week to
close-out for you? What completion
would give you the most satisfaction?
How can you finish your week and, in
some specific way, make the world a
little better than it was on Monday?

c3 _____

_____

_____

_____

_____ c03

I have written myself a
permission slip: It is okay to enjoy
these glorious spring days.

cs

cs

I honor the little girl inside who is jumping up and down shouting, "SNOW! SNOW! SNOW!"

ℭ _____

_____

_____

_____

_____ ℭ

I see the buds bursting with their irrepressible expression of self, and I wonder, what blooms within me?

ɔ᛭_____

_____

_____

_____

_____᛭ɔ

It's Friday! An ending, a beginning, neither or both? Whatever it is, can you find something to celebrate today? Identify it now. Look forward to it. Involve others. Today, celebrate!

� _____

_____

_____

_____

_____ ᛒ

On this longest night, as solstice promises the return of the light, I remember: "Sometimes it takes darkness and the sweet confinement of your aloneness to learn anything or anyone that does not bring you alive is too small for you" (from "Sweet Darkness," by David Whyte).

ଔ_____
_____
_____
_____
_____ଔ

Solstice reminds me to have faith in life's cycles, to believe, no matter how dark, that the light will return, and to submit to the certainty of my growth being called upward.

ൡ_____
_____
_____
_____
_____ൡ

Sunday evening: take a moment to align yourself mentally, physically and spiritually for the week ahead. Choose an empowering intention. Organize your schedule and your priorities. Identify an ideal that gives meaning to your work. Imagine the difference these few minutes can make!

cs _____

_____

_____

_____

_____ cs

The approaching new year is the most powerful time of the year to release the old and make way for the new. Spend some quiet time recognizing and appreciating your last year's successes, and envisioning next year's vision and goals. Consciously or not, you are now planting seeds you will soon harvest. You have the power to plant a garden you will enjoy.

Cʒ_____

_____

_____

_____

_____Cʒ

This special day reminds me to honor the common bonds that unite and connect us, and to celebrate the human capacity to hope.

ଓ_____

_____

_____

_____

_____ଓ

Saturday morning. A weekend yawning before me. If I could do ANYTHING with it, it would be . . .

附_____

_____

_____

_____

_____附

Sunday evening is the perfect time to shift gears. Look at the week ahead, your appointments and commitments, and decide what you would like to experience. What will this week hold for you? Name the joys, the successes, the connections, the opportunities . . .

 Cʒ _____

_____

_____

_____

_____ Cʒ

Here's Monday, with all its potential. Stop and imagine how you'd like this week to go. Write it here to increase your intention's power and energy. Believe it and you will receive it!

ᏣᏗ _____

_____

_____

_____

_____ ᏣᏗ

Day is ending. What had your attention today? What does it tell you about where your INTENTION should be tomorrow? A few minutes of review can completely redirect your experience.

 Cঽ_____

_____

_____

_____

_____Cঽ

December is no ordinary month. It is laden with memories and fears, hopes and anxieties, expectations and disappointments, and an exponential increase in To Do's. If you want to do more than "just get through it," an empowering, consciously-chosen intention will help. Take a moment to imagine, in detail, with specifics, your highest and best December. Proclaim it here and watch it unfold.

 C8 _____

_____

_____

_____

_____ C8

# CREATE YOUR OWN INTENTION

A new month—a new beginning—what would you like the next month to hold for you?

Ↄ_____

_____

_____

_____

_____Ↄ

As always, you will experience what you expect to experience today. Take a moment to envision positive and empowering interactions and outcomes.

CB_____

_____

_____

_____

_____CB

Can you think of an empowering thought you'd like to return your mind to over and over today?

 CB _____

_____

_____

_____

_____ CB

Clearing out fear, negativity and
scarcity-thinking, open your channels to
a glimpse of your highest possibilities
today . . . what do you see?

∞_____

_____

_____

_____

_____∞

Consciously set your intention today. Stop; get still for a moment. Imagine the challenges and opportunities the day ahead may hold for you. Now think of a statement that you can program into your mind to help you reach your highest potential. Feel free to proclaim it here. Enjoy your empowered day!

ೞ_____

_____

_____

_____

_____ೞ

Consider the day ahead, its challenges and opportunities, and think of a statement that can keep you focused on your highest, best self. What is it?

�_____

_____

_____

_____

_____ ᛫

Considering your schedule, the people you will encounter, the tasks you must complete, and the place you will go, what thought can you turn to, today, over and over to keep your spirit lifted, your sights high, and your heart true?

ೖ_____

_____

_____

_____

_____ೖ

Do you have a challenge, situation, effort or encounter ahead of you today that would benefit from a positive and empowering mental background? Paint your background now—decided your intention—so it will be there when you need it.

cx_____

_____

_____

_____

_____cx

Don't stop believing. Your dreams matter. What is important to you IS important. This is only a test. In the event of an actual emergency, you will be provided for. What "silly" dreams need to see the light of day?

ɔʒ_____

_____

_____

_____

_____ ɔʒ

Every experience begins with a thought.

Are you watching what you're thinking?

cs_____

_____

_____

_____

_____cs

Good news! This day holds gifts for you!
Little surprises to delight and inspire
you. Be curious. Be expectant. Be
grateful. What gifts are you receiving?

ଔ_____

_____

_____

_____

_____ଔ

How important it is for you to be your true, authentic self? If you don't be you and do what you came to earth to do, who will? Don't deprive the world of the gift that you were meant to bring. How will you be AUTHENTIC today?

CS _____

_____

_____

_____

_____ CS

If you had what you want,
what would your life look and feel like
today? Be specific—imagine and
describe your experience.

 C逢 _____

_____

_____

_____

_____ C逢

Imagine the highest and best

outcomes today. What will they be?

ങ_____

_____

_____

_____

_____ങ

Intention can seem illusive, just out of reach or sight. But it is there, in your heart, driving your choices and coloring your experiences, whether you see it or not. Take a moment to get clear on your intention today—what REALLY motivates you to do the things you do? Focus on the positive and empowering aspects that point you higher. Enjoy the beauty, joy and abundance that living with intention brings you!

ᘓ_____
_____
_____
_____
_____ᘓ

Is there a challenging situation
or relationship ahead of you today?
Take a moment to imagine the best
possible outcome. Anchor that picture
in your mind and go back to
it over and over today.

൭_____

_____

_____

_____

_____൭

Is your shadow seeking your attention? Today, notice where your impatience, irritation and anger with others is really about you seeing something in them that you don't like in yourself. Can you see it . . . forgive it . . . accept it . . . embrace it? Of course you can! If you decide to.

03_____

_____

_____

_____

_____03

Just as the Colorado River carved the Grand Canyon, you are constantly, little by little, shaping your life. What "little" things can you do differently today to shape it according to your deepest truths and highest callings?

ଓ3 _____

_____

_____

_____

_____ ଓ3

Let the noise die down. Let the
static settle. Hear the small, clear voice
inside that proclaims your greatness.
Hear it? It loves you and wants the
best for you. What does it say?

ᘓ_____

_____

_____

_____

_____ᘓ

Living with intention means taking responsibility for your thoughts, choosing thoughts that empower you. With 60,000+ thoughts per day, this can be hard to do. To make it more manageable, choose one empowering thought you can return your scattered thinking to over and over throughout the day. What empowering thought will work for you today?

છ _____

_____

_____

_____

_____ છ

Ok, your turn to experience
the power . . . name what you want
to experience today. Put it into words.
State it outloud. Write it here. Plant it in
your heart and mind. This is where all
experience begins, as a seed that takes
root and sprouts into reality.

What will you reap?

ဢ_____

_____

_____

_____

_____ ဢ

One of the clarifying questions of intention: Who do you really answer to? Who are you trying to please with the things you do and choices you make? What makes you keep going/doing no matter what? Get clear about that and you get closer to your true intention.

ೞ_____

_____

_____

_____

_____ೞ

Relax in the knowledge that
the Universe colludes for your
success. Imagine obstacles falling
away and resources appearing.
What is possible for you today?

ଔ_____

_____

_____

_____

_____ ଔ

Take a moment to think
of the day ahead. What thought can
you plant in your mind, and return to
over and over again, to support your
highest success and happiness? Increase
its energy by sharing it with someone.
Enjoy your wonder-full day!

CB _____

_____

_____

_____

_____ CB

Tell the world! What will you

make of this precious day?

᎒ß_____

_____:_____

_____

_____

_____᎒ß

Think about your life mission.
What experiences and abilities give
your life meaning? What do you
enjoy most? What do others seem to
appreciate most about you? Your
mission is not necessarily your vocation.
It fills the gaps in your thinking. It is
what your heart longs for. It is often too
obvious to see. What would happen
today if you made choices toward
fulfilling your life's mission?

CB _____

_____

_____

_____

_____ CB

Today contains a poem for you to discover. Pay attention—only you can give it life. Notice: words that vibrate in your heart; metaphors that surround you; the rhythm and cadence of events; insights that punctuate your awareness; meanings only you see. PAY ATTENTION to the poem being born through you today!

ଔ_____

_____

_____

_____

_____ ଔ

Today stretches before

you like an empty canvas.

How would you like to paint it?

cs_____

_____

_____

_____

_____ cs

Try this now: catch a negative thought or belief (inherently untrue) and turn it around to its positive, empowering truth. Feel your body release at the mere recognition of the truth. This is the subtle but powerful shift toward alignment. It feels good! Example: "I don't have time to do everything I need to do today" becomes "I have exactly enough time for the important things."

ᘓ_____

_____

_____

_____

_____ᘓ

What are your expectations
of today? Think about it. Whatever
you believe deep down inside, you
will experience. Take a moment to
make sure your expectations are
empowering and positive.

 catch_____

_____

_____

_____

_____catch

What do you want? I mean
REALLY want. Put it in words!!!
You must name it to claim it.

ᑦ _____

_____

_____

_____

_____ ᑦ

What is the single most important thing you can do/be today? Identify it now—write it down, even—so you'll remember it when the day's demands and distractions tempt your focus.

CB _____

_____

_____

_____

_____ CB

You know the way a song gets stuck in your head? That's the way conscious intention works. Choose meaningful and uplifting "lyrics" and play them over and over and over. It completely changes your day!

ℭ_____

_____

_____

_____

_____ ℭ

You will decide your experiences today—not the things that happen, perhaps, but how you respond to them. Decide now: what will you experience today?

ભ_____

_____

_____

_____

_____ભ

Your day is an empty vase.

What flowers will you put in it?

CB_____

_____

_____

_____

_____CB

Your lover surrounds you with gifts. Each moment is rich with them. Be a gracious receiver. Your needs are met. Your desires are provided for. Your comfort is assured. Soak in the gifts of your all-knowing, all-powerful Lover. Know that you are loved.

୯ß_____

_____

_____

_____

_____୯ß

Your thoughts create your experience. Make sure even your oldest, deepest, most basic beliefs support your highest possibilities. Try this . . . finish this sentence in an empowering way and say it to yourself 100 times today:

"I am _____."

ଓ _____

_____

_____

_____

_____ ଓ

CB_____

_____

_____

_____

_____CB

# About the Author

EMPOWERMENT EXPERT, TRANSFORMATIONAL trainer, and whole-being, well-being whiz, Liz Garrett, is shifting lives with creative, reality-based programs that work on all levels—mind, body and spirit—for deep and lasting change in individuals and organizations. A successful business owner since 1998, and having worked collaboratively with execs for more than 20 years, she knows well the fire inside that either propels you to greatness, or consumes you in the effort. Find out more at www.TrueYouAdvantage.com.

Liz is Virginia born and raised, and still there. She prefers "y'all" for second-person plural, can slurp her weight in Chesapeake Bay oysters and, if she says to you, "Bless your heart," that's not necessarily a good thing.

Thank you for reading this book.

I appreciate your feedback and love hearing your thoughts, stories and experiences with the material, and suggestions for the next version.

Please leave a helpful review at Amazon.

Yours in wellness, purpose and abundance,

—Liz Garrett

# Do You Have a Book to Write?

SELF-PUBLISHING
SCHOOL

Discover the EXACT 3-step blueprint you need to become a bestselling author in 3 months.

Self-Publishing School helped me, and now I want them to help you with this FREE VIDEO SERIES!

Even if you're busy, bad at writing, or don't know where to start, you CAN write a bestseller and build your best life.

With tools and experience across a variety of niches and professions, Self-Publishing School is the only resource you need to take your book to the finish line.

DON'T WAIT!

Watch this FREE VIDEO SERIES now,
and say "YES" to becoming a best seller:

Watch the First Video at
https://xe172.isrefer.com/go/sps4fta-vts/EWC001

Made in the USA
Columbia, SC
24 April 2020